Adult Head

A Nightingale Edition

Adult Head

Poems by Jeff Tweedy

Zoo Press

The author thanks the editors of the following journals in which some of these poems first appeared, sometimes in slightly different forms:

Ecstatic Peace: "Breaking News," "Prayer #5" and "White Kitten Snowcone Two"; *Lit:* "When I Say My Heart," "At Night," "*Ein Moment,*" "Kitten Epic," and "Easy Bake Oven"; *Painted Bride Quarterly:* "Pure Bug Beauty" and "Prayer #3"; *Unpleasant Event Schedule:* "Prayer #1," "Another Great Thing," "I Am One of You," and "Why the Hat."

Zoo Press • P.O. Box 22990 • Lincoln, Nebraska 68542
Printed in the United States of America

Distributed to the trade by The University of Nebraska Press
Lincoln, Nebraska 68588 • www.nebraskapress.unl.edu

Cover design by Janice Clark of Good Studio © 2004
www.goodstudio.com

Library of Congress Cataloging-in-Publication Data

Tweedy, Jeff, 1967–
  Adult head : poems / by Jeff Tweedy.-- 1st ed.
     p. cm.
  ISBN 1-932023-16-X (pbk. : alk. paper)
  I. Title.
  PS3620.W44A67 2004
  811'.54--dc22

                                         2004002254

zoo020 / night001

First Edition

Table of Contents

1

2

3

For my brother Steve,
for introducing me to the word

1

Satan Explains

there is no fire in my fireplace
there is no time left to understand
the fortunes of these minor souls
I have replaced my disorders
with a passion so deep and pervasive
to never sleep the fugitive-sleep again
the guns are going off
the rockets exploding
the jambs splintering
the life unfolding
the dreams
to gaze undaunted into this
miserable play
again and again
recombine
elope to finer cuts of grass
steal away to softer skin
hold tighter those objects
charged and bleeding

the path greater loves have hardened
walk slowly and persist

let's wear momentum
how honor pulverizes this now
like nothing else
it's happening
so loosen your body
to me

Singing Combat

just as you approach...a package
pulling at its bow, I see your face
retreating from singing combat
from falling down a flight of stairs
our good days, our parents old, radiant beauty
back there behind the sunshine

I believe your sorrow was sunshine
murdered for longing, your broken package
a crushed open can of a pure bug's beauty
crawling up lip and lash on your face
before afternoon smiled for climbed stairs
all because your laugh suggested combat

it seems worthwhile to wish for combat
steadying knees knotting in the sunshine
bracing knuckles unskinned on stairs
where the tree-lit pattern and wrapped package
conceals no thoughtless purchase of your face
and kills no surprise of beauty

attacked by love laughing with beauty
the four winds blow and the brave combat-
ants have no weapons, no face
no fear, no mirror to hurt sunshine
they pry to know this ticking package
but none can climb so many soft stairs

they fall in heaps at the bottom of these stairs
wounded and comforted only by beauty
they come tangled in twine to tie this package
and limping away whisper combat
and say later it was a somewhat shaded sunshine
approaching along with your face

and the starlight we're running to face
scales slowly twisting the stairs
how love stops blood in sunshine
not worth the fight but for beauty
we will all go far away from this singing, combat
and become ourselves armored packages

to face sunlight, starlight, sunshine
packaged with beautiful notes scaling stairs
you are not above saying combat

When I Say My Heart

I mean
an emergency
worse than a clarinet

or an old man who just won't
stand out of the way

I don't mean a parking lot
but the pretty twisting oil slick

the waving arms
of awful drinking

false teeth

an unpopular child
on a swing set
or the least wanted crayon

sometimes I mean
a foil moon

checkpoint charlie
or a ghost

or sitting duck

Prayer #1

a bouquet of disasters
to be grown

the orchestra
is proving the dead again

red flashes are
the bells ringing

hide with me
alive in the weeds

the flowers paused
are the fury
and dead song, waiting...

Unlikely Japan

when I say that she's the rapist
that really isn't what I mean
it was all in my imagination
to be claimed too easily

with almost loving force of will
what would have been given sadly
without deceiving me with skill
she was still only taking
what I should give more carefully

(but now) religion enters in
god cracks through her moist skin
and twirls from her baton
her hair suggests a roller skate

he whispers through her perfume
just above shallow watery surfaces
ripples with actions lovelike
there is no voice so thin

she knows what she wants
that she wants what she knows
she wants this to mean nothing and that sounds fair to me
a made-by-hand halo and new-fashioned wings

she is blind to be an angel that's rare to be
she's not so well rounded
she has points you don't see
she does whatever she wants
(and I swear)
she wanted me

Another Great Thing

the best way
to feel your blood
is to lie

tell bold lies
about books
(even better)
say
you write

listen,
lying won't help at all
unless,
you pick the right people

people who know
how to write and lie

o, and then the blood will pound
discoteque-esque
otherwise
it won't at all

Pure Bug Beauty

I attack with love
folded, my wings
crawl up to you
and your afternoon
I've been puking

you move so slow
a steady crushing hand
over my body
a company
in my back

hide your soft skin
your sorrow in sunshine
listening to my eyes
they are full
of bloodful tunes

you learn so slow
old fleshy beauty
I curve my flight
under your bent knee
I will always die

so you can remember me

Poison Color

we had to invent the poison color
the color poison
the venomous hue
because we had spent all the roads between the roads
and society must keep its figure
because we had other solutions but they wouldn't admit they had problems
because we had already accomplished love
and the furnace kept freezing
the flowers had paused
because no one could remember how not to talk in the third person
and we needed the rest

The Black Hours

—G M H

are almost gone
the night is dissolving
in a cup of god lifted
to toast the lightning
lightly tapping
high-pitched as it hums

and as your spine shines
with your soul, a shiver,
a fist so clear and trying
to climb into the unlit sky
you can see
there's so much less to this than you think

your mind's a machine
that's deadly and dull
it's never been still
and its will has never been free
it's almost dawn
and it's snowing again

I have never seen so much night

Prayer # 2

when dogs laugh barking
I say angry
some say laughing
they don't stop and they smile
we are sure they can't get us
bite us
but I think the fence does nothing
and that's why they are laughing
and they bark because they know

At Night

in the southern galaxy
at the tip of the letter *k*
I'm afraid to look at moving pictures

in the jukebox din
scratched to silence
breaking bread

I hide from the flux of time
the burning light
funneled into perfect holes

I'm content to know
that I'm not a spot of unsung melody
afraid to look at moving pictures

I Am One of You

I am one
stupid-
looking book,
a thick song
too tired
to half-talk
corner me
the window–way
out of the object
with only
this to say

and this will sing to you
or write around you
outlined in
the mirror–way,
a chalk performance

Blueheart Chrome

temper is the day long
in white robes
I loathe this troubled mind
hovering over my skull

swindling and swindled
half-happy to know
jesus what I am not
a spot
of unsung melody

in the southern galaxy
at the tip of a written word
afraid to look
at pictures moving

the flux of time
an un-imagined wheat field
of forgiveness systems
the rays of focused burning light
funneled in holes

translated poetry
for a blue calloused heart
neighboring seething songs
feeling what is good inside me

also holding bread
breaking the brain
in jukebox din
scratched to silence

while the attendant stares
talking about last night's episode
of the parrot ghost
or I'm an idiot

or I'm smart
so I gave up the
walk, singing
drunk on science

the stuff the kind pirates drink
I discovered her
super structure looming
goddess at thirty-two

why is it taking my voice so long...

Ein Moment

the peach colored payphone
in a bathroom in Munich
is calling America selfishly

the self-styled warlock
with tincture of lotus
holding a hand-held recorder

to my beak—I'm an interviewee
as if to say *this is important*
now I know you're not listening

this is what love is for

Capital City

in a capital city skyline photo
skyscrapers shine with sun
low in the blue sky

but the secretaries at the hot dog vendors
and the car horns honking at bicycle messengers
make no reply

I can't call with a subway token
besides the phones are all broken
I wish you were here, or I was there with you

you wouldn't like it here
you better stay there
a breath in the country air

as I consider if it's unfair
no longer pretending I care
why I should wait for you

Way of Light (Christmas, 1978)

arrive slow keep driving
turn off your lights even
if it's well before sundown
keep the windows up, locked
look at the outlines of wise men
two dimensional and flat
see the shepherds and of course
Jesus would be beautiful
this is the way of light
and we are here mid-day
we see the wires and plastic bulbs
the guts of light
and where the light would be shining
if it could be shining
if there was darkness
instead we idle almost
toward thousands of candles
a shrine unlit no flames
and a grotto of poured painted cement
where I assume people pray
so we can speed away then

2

Christmas, 1978, Later

paper piles up Christmas on the carpet
glossed printed rolled cut folded taped fingerprinted
torn rippled ripped smashed fisted into balls
degifted

Sister Invention

I invented a sister
populated her confession
with knives
encouraged her crown
colored her disagreeable
taught her town jokes
but she was poisoned by the earth
and she had
luggage with ladders
so I let her search the roads
between the roads
where she got lost
and finally moved away

Laughs

the greatest songs
are never sung
but the grass
gets cut
and spelled
in children's hands
how the sun is yellow
but also cold and sutured
...blue

the best laughs
never leave your lungs
and the best life
is art
never made

Kitten Epic

seeing not so well
falsetto failing
and irregular
chasing children
like an epic
the kitten
epic
upon freeing
breaking away from
the motorcade
finds us both
lonely for a throne

where the waves
are pewter
blankets of dull
silver motion

This is New

this is new
this is
the new
the new me
the new them
the new us
this is

the path
greater love has hardened

walk slowly

persist

wear the momentum
care less
honor only this

nothing else
can happen
to my body

Yachting?

I have never been yachting
or on a boat
but
I imagine it
a passionate bath
with an older brother
gentle then turning
competitive
as he studies
for the bar

Damen Avenue

six kids down the street
I am thinking automatically (six kids down)

she touches the outside
of every boy she climbs on (and climbs off)

countless kids across
the city–street–smile

silent pistons beat
crushing our hearts (street success)

there's nobody listening
my suspicion is this

the hardest part is
shaking the tongue (sweetness gone)

is it fiction because
someone said it was so

because someone said
it was love (functional)

please don't ever
fall for that (I hope I hope)

here it is like this
her parents split

Prayer #3

I have pondered
the long unpublished poems
of someone's only son
that dead laugh
spun over stone
where french-kissed teenaged girls blush
and flash teasing tooth-pouts
lasting moments less
than real hope stirring
symphonic shouts
again slack
in service of dread,
mocked continents drifting
stems already shooting
across time's seamlessness
I have enjoyed these hours more
with you not by my side

I'm a Wheel

I'm a wheel
I will...................turn on you

hold on
                    you risk exciting me

once in Germany someone said *nein*!
once in Germany someone said *nein*!

hold back
                    don't invite me

hold your breath
and count to nine

'm a wheel
I will...................shine

I invented a sister
                    populated with knives

hang up and call my other line
once in Germany someone said *nein*

fall backwards and count to nine
what's this attack

I am will and I turn
                    on you, turn on you

I will feel you and you
will...................feel me shine

Half-Pill

the roof held its charm
tight against the rising
orange half-pill
the moon and myself
a sculpture
and my ear
a shy sculpture
smashed against a phone
receiving the static
and my son's
tutelage
in a moment of art
a translation
lost forever

This Child

toward the end
of an emergency
worse than a universe
of musical instruments
an old man
stood out of the way
and watched
time's distortion of oil
the awful waving appendages
of false teeth
drinking
pivoting with his laugh
one child is not popular
a front line drawn in crayon
knows how to kill the feel
of a swing set
impresses a broken tooth
into the face of his mother
and fills it
with moons of foil

Easy Bake Oven

I wish I could
move you like a millionaire
however I please
make you sing
chocolate cupcakes and other
teen recipes

I wish I could
move you like a millionaire
remember what you made
a poet down on my knees
spray-painted pink shoes
filling up all your pans
you made stink

I wish I could
fuck you like he thinks he does
before he falls asleep
but I've never been that tired
and I've never been too sad
to eat

White Kitten Snow Cone Two

no one
will tell you

you are not
a rainbow

but the white kitten
is a snow cone

blank ice frozen
flavored water

awaiting
the thick syrup, great

and sickening
self

with no where
to vibrate

but in you
through you

sculpted, still
air decides

how long
back to air

Prayer #4

to be a saint
you need to have everything
rigid speech
leading nowhere
as little as we are
saints need to be smaller
actually on the page
looking up stupid
not just words
ink

3

First This

I'm full but not finished
with a first thought
I know now
I speak kindness
but a darkness holds
the shy apology
in my heart

also, I know first thoughts
last traveled along
my keyless skull
to make me now a father
to my father
as you were to your mother
a mother

on the playground
many things passed me by
until the first hard word
left my lips
a fist to myself
outside myself
watching myself
hating
myself
fitting in

Knives and Forks

knives and forks
perform over my bed

fiberglass insulation,
a migrating pink dream

saying
pull the broken brake
hard
pulse it
quicken the
slip

someone was right
training drinks
to feel like school

broad with information

pressing for more,
forming bruises

where (into this drawer)
I am waking

Study

from the valley
toward the mountain
(you get there)
through the valley
(you go) eyes down
a flash
a stream
golden and small
relentless and understood
(you find things)
and then the hills
you know they are in front of you
and behind you
what's behind is erased
they are there
small and they are
all you see
beyond maybe mountains
but for now
to have at least an
incline, steady slopes
back to the valley
study it before the
hills now you're sure they exist
is there something here
that will help you climb?
was it worn
have you missed
the valley arrangements of
smaller deserts and
microscopic deaths
less and less evolving

giants zoomed in
focus on plants
and the life you can't name
you know they have names
forget the mountain
the depths of dreaming
and the valley and
feel each foot fall
and the climb
and ignore the peak
surrender just fall softly
and let the petrified
be destroyed
and destroy

War is Coming

to be near you soon

I can see the stretchers
from a Hilton in Adelaide
eleventh floor
tiny teeth closing
on the horizon
almost invisible

not hiding
even the sea

right here in our city
we have room
for seventy of them
patients for our
white and black
overweight nurses
well designed
triple failures
pocketing the pills
bedside

The Bench-Warmer's Daughter

the poor devil is living some psycho-somatic Beethoven com-
plex selected from memory. he can't hear. not even his own
bleating. maintaining a steady diet of tunes nonetheless deaf. it
only took him a year to learn how to read. poetry starting to
blink out from under a dull gray cap. he ate the heavy greased
song and it tasted like all he'd ever known. everything else tast-
ed like thin air. per diem. laid out platters of shit so vile, john-
ny john johns, drawl-boy and the new-kid would stuff their
guts and feel it burning in their necks and flushing down their
pink apple cheeks and piss it with cold beer. all equations and
measured intersections droned and dutifully finished his
melodies. now there wasn't time left for you-knife-who. she...
she dissipated the last of his adult head and good night, rode
off over the phone lines that reeled in him jerks and pulls
scraping the finished gloss of an imagined book-style master-
piece. he could hear her. was he or would he ever again be
warming benches?

Breaking News

every house
is dark
coming down
coatless
energy
sliding open
black a dim yellow light
enters the gospel
flooding my contented
little radio

Muzzle

there's a random
painted highway
and a muzzle of bees
my sleeves have come unstitched
from climbing your tree

the sun gets passed from tree to tree
silently and back to me
a breeze blown through
pushed up above the sea
finally next to you

when dog's bark they look like they're smiling
I don't think they're mean
some people get frightened
despite fences in between
and the green gets passed...

to you as you begin to cry
I said maybe if I leave
you'll want me to come home
or maybe all you mean
is to sting a silence in me

you're irresistible when you get mad
isn't it sad I'm immune
and I thought it was cute
for you to kiss my purple black eye
even though I caught it from you

I still think we're serious

Doris

let's start in the room
where we were born
the irons were hot
overused and underslept
like doris
the women
the daughter of
the woman next door
she was crazy
she hadn't bought clothes
in twenty years
she held her shirts together
with big yarn stitches
and safety pins
her glasses
had only one arm
we weren't allowed
to wear red
when we played
in the backyard
because it inspired
worse than normal fits
she saw the devil
in anything red
she also saw
the sirens that
often came
to take her
back to the sanitarium
her mother would
show up
in our yard

timidly knocking
bloodied from *falls*
down the basement stairs
when she died
they took doris
away forever
and she died
sooner than that

Prayer #5

the snow is making
frying sounds
like an enormous
audience of glass
and paper hands
we can tune this out
unlike the woods
early black spill
or our engines

Temper, Temper

temper is honey
I see cars crashing, a cop flashing
I turn the TV off

the heart is a hollow fist
on mornings like this
there isn't enough to believe

home isn't satisfaction,
retroaction,
is this feeling your arms

remember your temper, honey
you're not the only one loving
living raw, hovering...

is a white, scalding robe,
a laughter passing in strobes,
welcome it again

one sees it after dark
the small glowing arc
of moonshine behind you

temper remembers you, honey
and the bees have stopped stinging
as we keep coming home

which isn't cars crashing,
isn't light flashing
isn't this feeling I'm having in your arms

Why the Hat

I caught a glimpse of myself
in a closed circuit television screen

I was wearing a hat
a fraud
a punctured white watch

I hadn't changed

The Next Ten Years

I want to begin
where the dilation charges
and juries weep
over half-opened wombs.
Where god staggers in
cleft chinned and brooding
dizzy, sick with creation.
I want to begin with this,
minus infinity.

Hell

When the devil came
he was not red
but chrome
and he said
come with me
you must go
so I went
alone
where there was no fire
no torture
no hate
everything clean and precise
towering polished diamond skyscrapers
glittering ice avenues
translucent blues and silver signs
marking every turn
I was welcomed
with open arms
unmarked
all lines of defeat sanded away
I felt no fear
I received every kind of help
the air was crisp
sunny late winter days
springtime yawning
over the cottony horizon
hell is chrome
I believe in god
hell is chrome